Turtle Creek House

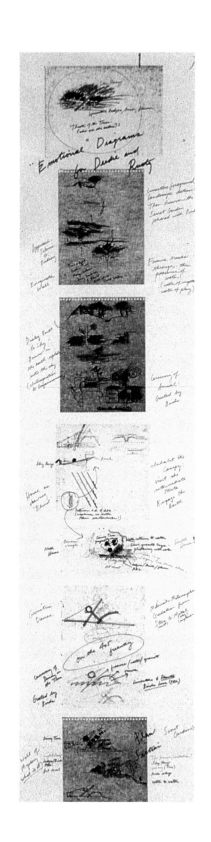

THE MONACELLI PRESS

Turtle Creek House

Antoine Predock

Introduction by Antoine Predock

Architect	Antoine Predock Architect
Principal	Antoine Predock
Project Team	John Brittingham
	Geoffrey Beebe
	Jorge Burbano
	Paul Gonzales
	David Nelson
Interior Furnishings	Emily Summers
	Mil Bodron
Structural Consultant	James F. Smith
Mechanical/Electrical Consultant	MEP Systems Design & Engineering
Landscape Consultant	Rosa Finsley
Contractor	Thos. S. Byrnc, Inc.

First published in the United States of America in 1998 by
The Monacelli Press, Inc.,
10 East 92nd Street, New York, New York 10128.

Library of Congress Cataloging-in-Publication Data
Turtle Creek House : Antoine Predock / introduction by Antoine Predock.
    p.   cm.—(One house)
ISBN 1-885254-48-2
1. Turtle Creek House (Dallas, Tex.). 2. Architecture, Modern—20th century—Texas—Dallas.
3. Dallas (Tex.)—Buildings, structures, etc. 4. Predock, Antoine—Criticism and interpretation.
I. Predock, Antoine. II. Series.
NA7238.D2T87 1997
728'.37'097642812—dc21   97-39006

Printed and bound in Italy

Designed and edited by *Group* C Inc. New Haven/Boston

Turtle Creek Contents

6

Introduction

Antoine Predock

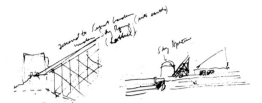  

The site seemed somewhat unlikely for clients who were avid bird-watchers: a cul-de-sac off a busy Dallas street serving a small neighborhood of relatively traditional houses. Leaving the street and moving into the site, the motivation for its selection becomes clear—the verdant realm of the Turtle Creek watershed, a habitat for birds at the convergence of two major continental flyways. This connection to the natural realm was critically important.

Literally at the end of the cul-de-sac, the site opened to the creek, with the plane of the water substantially lower than the level of the street. The trees on the site engendered a real sense of enclosure and containment, a sense of mystery—one could gaze toward the other side of the creek through the filtered light of the forest canopy. Below the canopy, the ground plane plunged down to the level of the water with white limestone outcrops that defined the edge of the creek. It was a sylvan, almost magical landscape.

My instinct was to contain the site with the house and not let that sense of magic and power be released toward the street. The site would be discovered incrementally from the street approach—one would leave the world of the street behind and enter the realm of the watershed.

Located on the highest ground of the site, the house appears, from the street side, to be embedded in the earth. One first encounters five massive limestone ledges—a dam of expectations. This weighty, earth-bound foreground, a geologic parallel to the Austin Chalk Formation, a

primary stratum running north-south through Dallas, suggests a time-less relationship to the site. Though somewhat softened by native Texas grasses and wildflowers planted to attract birds, the dominant impression of the ledges is solidity. This reading is reinforced by the cast-in-place concrete planes—the retaining walls that project out of and above the limestone ledges. This all but windowless facade, with its two-inch horizontal glass slits, is also a climatic response to the site—the ledges protect the hot, or west, side of the house.

There is a paradoxical sense of impenetrability that these ledges engender in the experience of encountering the house. They are a discrete barrier that one must pass through. The mute limestone is fractured by the entry fissure, which not only reveals the interior spaces but also creates a connection to the creek and trees on the other side.

Extending the axis of the entry fissure into the sky is the skyramp, a black steel structure that projects 40 feet above the site to arrive at the treetops. It establishes a trajectory from earth to sky, a connection between the weighty, ground-borne sense of the ledges—and the implication that they might even be growing from a substrate of that same material—and the visual weightlessness of the skyramp. This is an important symbolic reading that one cannot escape on entering the house. It is almost as though you enter the house and are immediately swept through to the realm beyond—a journey that is facilitated by the open, completely glazed arrival zone. This encounter, this "arrival," has nothing to do with the functioning of the house in a planning sense;

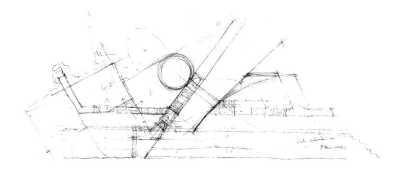

the encounter is with the timeless site.

The arrival zone and entry fissure split the house into two sections, two dominant zones: a north house and a south house. It is here that the strata of the house overlap, that the multiple paths through the house are visible: to the left, the kitchen and the north house; straight ahead and up the stairs, the dining tower and skyramp; to the right and up the broad concrete steps, the entertainment areas and, continuing up the narrower maple steps, the master suite; to the right and down, the subterranean gallery with the guest bedrooms and the small spiral stair that reconnects each level of the south house. Each path provides its own set of options, allowing one to set off on other paths and observe what is occurring elsewhere—within the house, and externally. On one level, the house has to do with contemplative personal connections to the landscape; on another, it is an extroverted social venue.

Embracing the site, the house to the south develops sectionally and horizontally. The excavation of the south-axis circulation zone, over which a portion of the living room cantilevers, serves the children's and guest bedrooms. This zone establishes an earthbound tie around which the sweep of glass and mirror of the living area spins—like a tether and the arc described by the end of a string whipping around.

The arced glazing of the living area shifts from an introspective focus into the core of the house to, at the other extreme, the expansive view of the city lights through the trees. From the vantage point of the lawn,

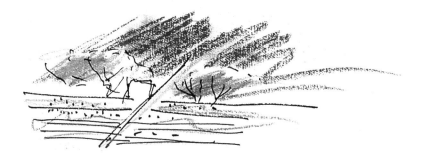

east of the house, looking back, inserted in the arcing sweep of the living area glazing, is a 20-by-20 convex polished stainless steel mirror. This piece reflects the house in a distorted fashion that challenges the stability of the viewer's position.

There is a purely phenomenological impulse toward the use of that convex mirror—how light strikes it and the juxtaposition of this opaque mirror with the transparent, yet mirrorlike, quality of the living area glazing. Overlaying that intention, though, is the compressed and distorted reflection of the house; is this reality or is the presumed physicality of the house reality? This notion of dematerialization and destabilization, in a polemical not a perverse way, is part of the intention of the mirrored piece. It is also a kind of nature proscenium when viewed from the exterior. And, viewed from within, its weightlessness is underscored by the surrounding glazing, which floats the wall above the living area floor. In contrast to the wide open glazing that opens out to the creek and the city lights beyond, are the two-inch-wide horizontal slits that filter and project west light, particularly during sunset, onto surfaces within the house while defining wall and ceiling junctures.

The black steel trajectory established by the skyramp recurs as linkage within the arrival zone of the house where a lateral bridge connects the living area to the dining tower. Flanking the skyramp and emerging from the base of the dining tower is a prowlike terrace of cast-in-place concrete containing a sliver of turf.

The roofscape of the house is another habitable zone, and is

accessed directly from the dining tower and master suite. Developed sectionally, it echoes the internal volumetric displacements, the level changes within. This alternate topography provides an additional path through the house with its own events, including a rooftop gathering area with views to the treetops and back into the interior of the house through a glass oculus at the center of the dining tower. From that rooftop esplanade, one can view the ledges up close—as well as arriving guests and the sunset beyond.

The topographic roofscape bridges the earthbound arrival experience and the dance of the ephemeral skyramp and reflective arc. This house has very different personalities—from earthbound to flying on the end of a string. The roofscape puts a "lid" on it all; and the succession of levels provides varied view aspects between those extremes—sometimes the connection to the natural realm is close and intimate, and other times, farther away.

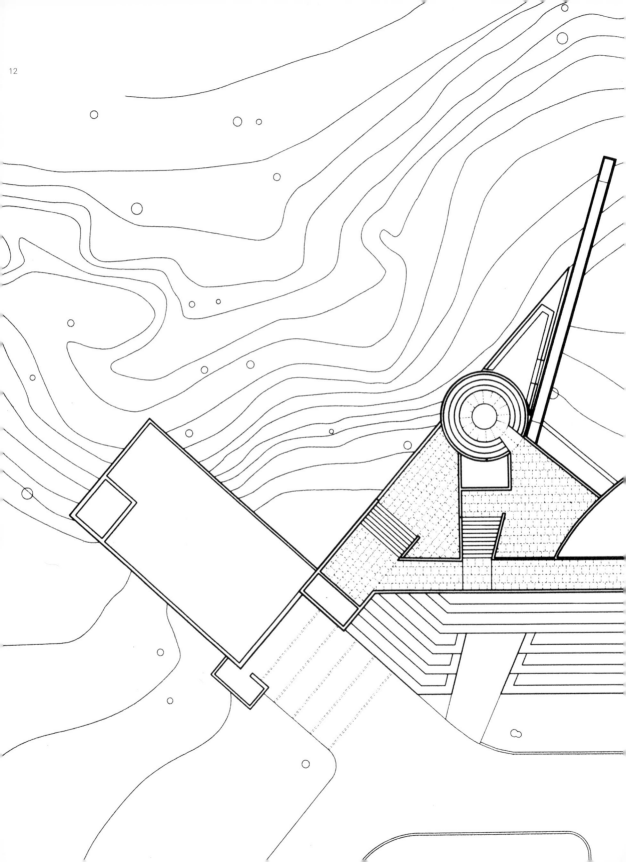

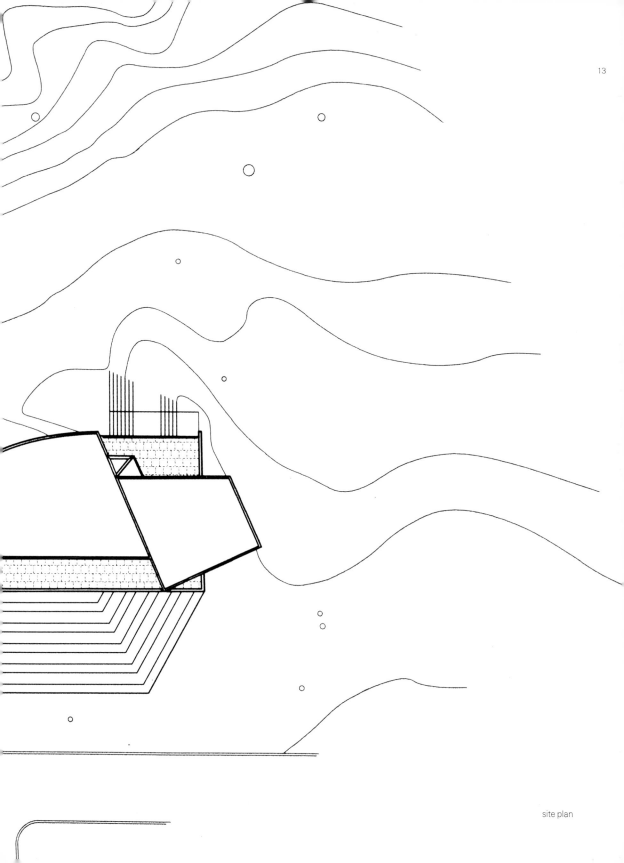

site plan

A ⌐

B ⟩ C

D ⌐

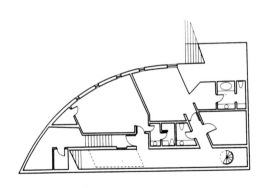

D ⌐

⟨ C

A ⌐

B ∨

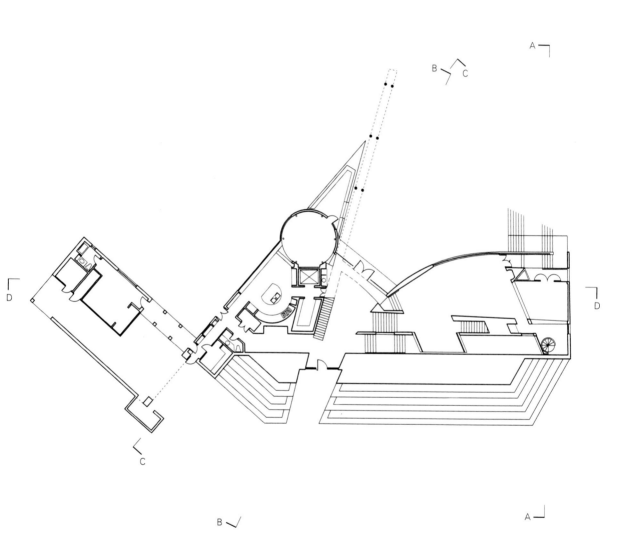

A

B ⌐ C

D

D

C

B

A

entry level

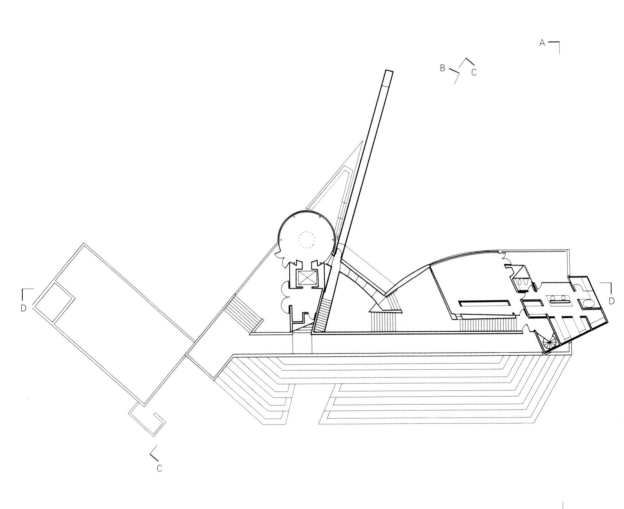

A

B C

D D

C

B

A

upper level

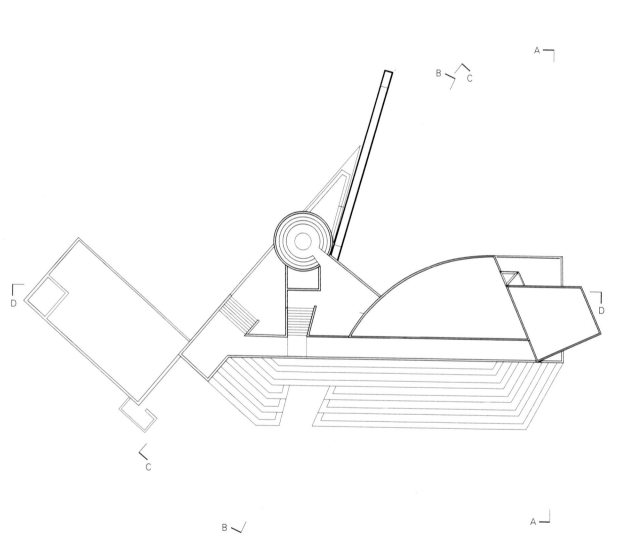

A ⌐

B ⌐ C

D ⌐

D ⌐

C ⌐

B √

A ⌐

roof

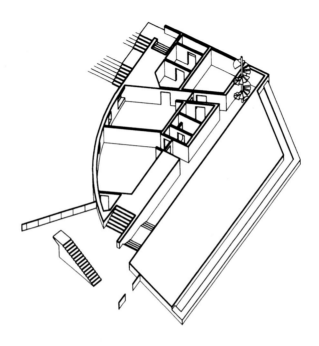

lower level axonometric

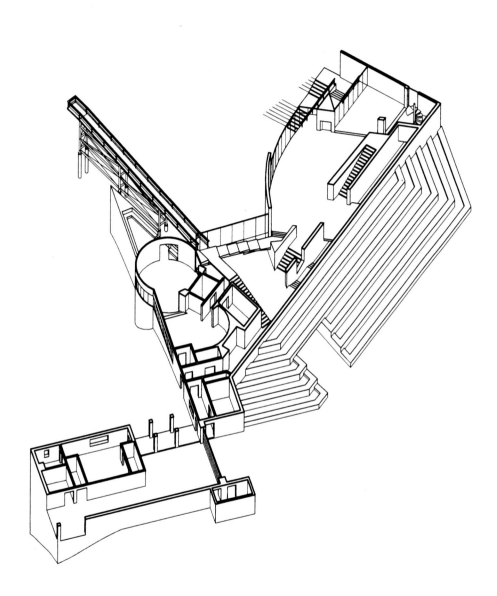

entry level axonometric

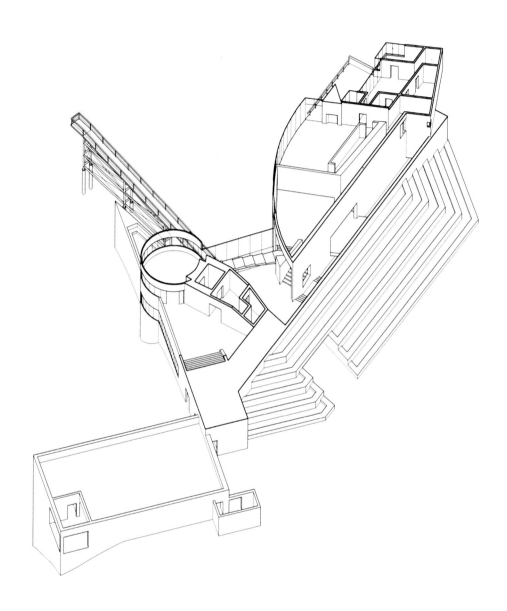

upper level axonometric

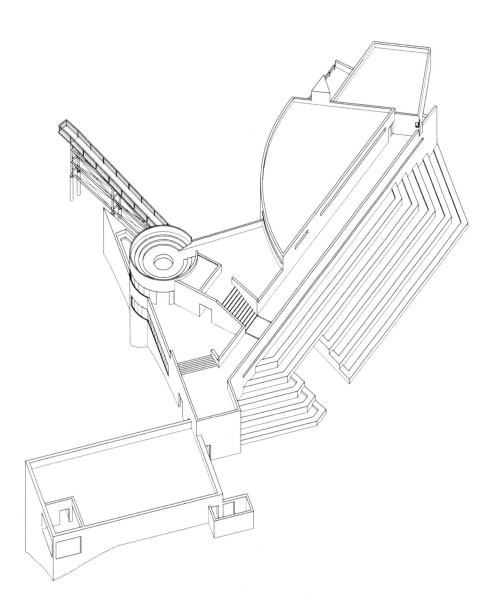

roof axonometric

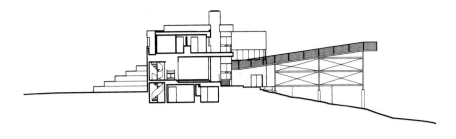

section AA

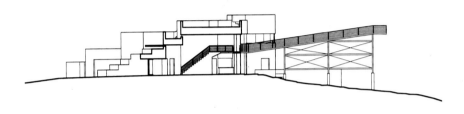

section BB

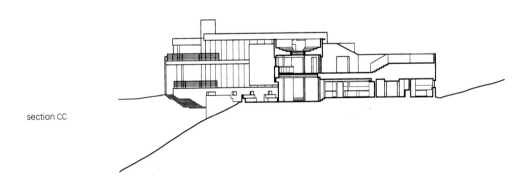

section CC

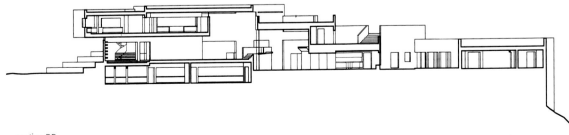

section DD

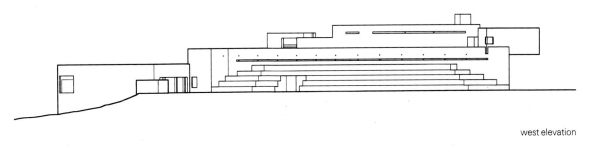

west elevation

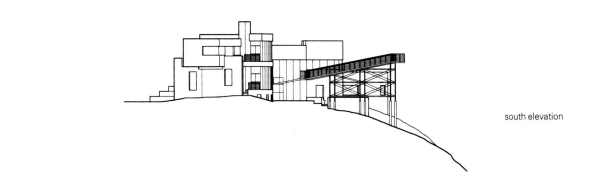

south elevation

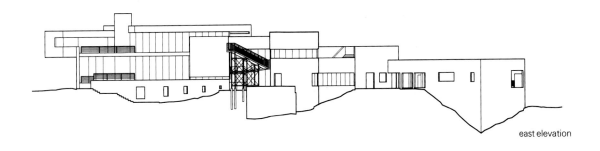

east elevation

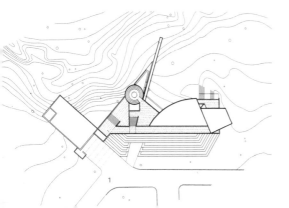

1

1 west facade from street

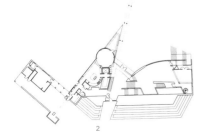

2

2 entry fissure through limestone ledges **3** foyer with stair to sky ramp

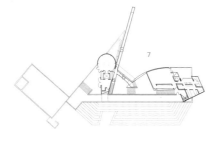
7

4 bridges to sky ramp **5** sky ramp **6** sky ramp/dining tower **7** east facade with stainless steel mirror (overleaf)

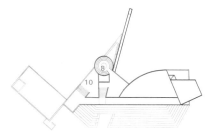
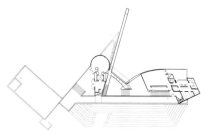

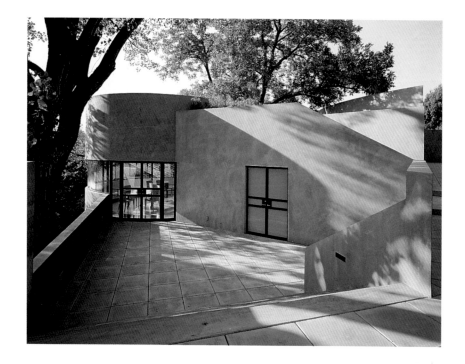

8 dining tower with oculus **9** roof terrace with oculus **10** roof terrace off dining tower

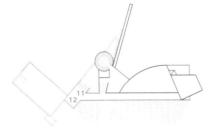

11, 12 roof terraces/limestone ledges

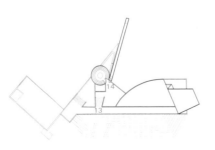

13 stair to upper roof terrace **14,15** roof amphitheater/oculus

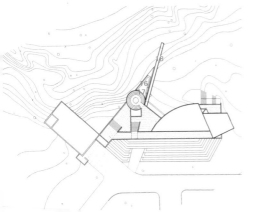

16, 17 prow terrace/sky ramp **18** sky ramp/dining tower

19, 20, 21 convex stainless steel mirror

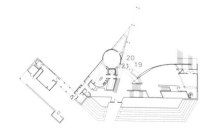

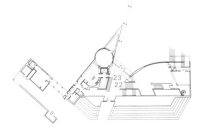

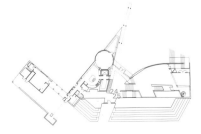

24 stair to living space, lower gallery **25** stair to living space

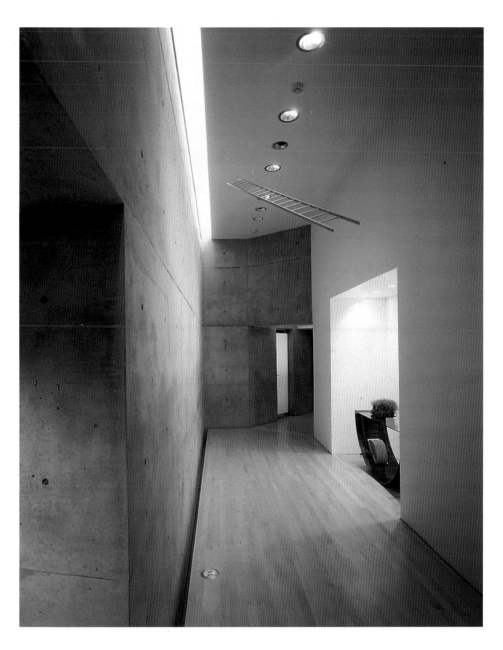

27 upper gallery

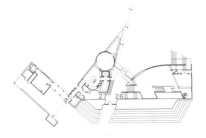

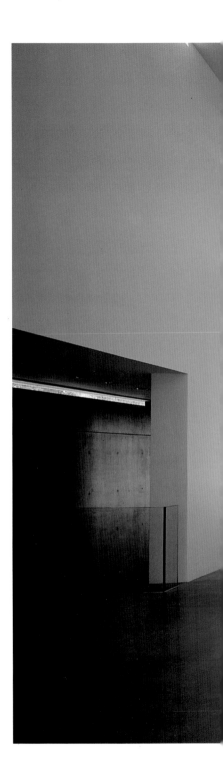

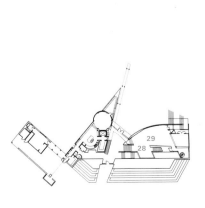

30 west cantilevered living area **31** west living area with stair to master suite

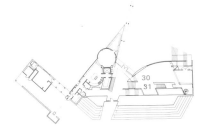

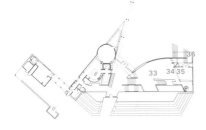

37 lawn from southeast **38** sky ramp from south **39** birdhouse

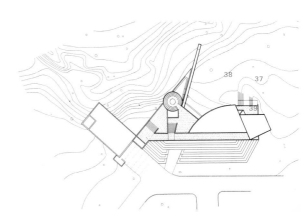

40 master suite **41** top of spiral stair **42** entry from master suite

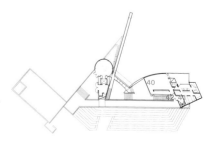

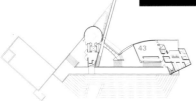

43 entry from master suite

44 stair to skyramp with kitchen doors **45** looking west toward entry doors

46

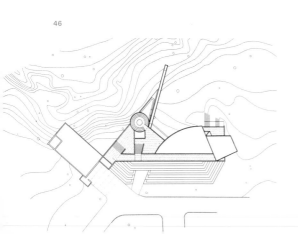

Photography Credits

Numbers refer to image numbers except as noted.

© **Scott Frances/Esto** 24, 32, 39, 40, 41, 43

© **Kirk Gittings/Syntax** page 11

© **Timothy Hursley** page 5, 4, 17, 18, 20–22, 28, 29, 42

© **Robert Reck** 1, 5, 8, 9–14, 16, 23, 25, 27, 30, 33, 37, 38, 44, 46

Robert Reck 2, 3, 6, 7, 15, 19, 26, 31, 34, 35, 36, 45
Courtesy of Architectural Digest. © 1994 The Condé Nast Publications. All rights reserved